PLANET UNDER PRESSURE

Too Many People on Earth?

Matt Anniss

W

FRANKLIN WATTS

LONDON•SYDNEY

First published 2015 by Franklin Watts
338 Euston Road
London NW1 3BH

Franklin Watts Australia
Level 17/207 Kent Street
Sydney, NSW 2000

Produced by Calcium

A CIP catalogue record for this book is available from
the British Library.

ISBN 978 1 4451 3872 5

Dewey classification: 363.9

Printed in China

Franklin Watts is a division of Hachette Children's Books,
an Hachette UK company
www.hachette.co.uk

Acknowledgements:
The publisher would like to thank the following for permission to reproduce
photographs: Dreamstime: Aedal 44, Antartis 43, Bgupal 39, Djembe 45,
Eprom 37, Hungchungchih 36, Jca 22, Sadikgulec 24, 25, Samrat35 34,
35, Urosr 42, Wollwerth 32; Shutterstock: 197lyes 11, ARENA Creative
41, Arindambanerjee 1, 17b, Hector Conesa 23, Sam D Cruz 17t, DP
Photography 10, Rob van Esch 31, Vladislav Gurfinkel 12, Homeros 9, 16,
Image Point Fr 38, Kaetana 18, Kataleewan Intarachote 8, Julius Kielaitis
28, Landmark Media 40, Meunierd 4, Mikeledray 26, Monkey Business
Images 7, Anton Oparin 29, Orange Line Media 15, Chris P. 13, Patrick
Poendl 33, Paul Prescott 19, Lev Radin 27, TonyV3112 5, Dana Ward cover,
Jaren Jai Wicklund 6, Steshkin Yevgeniy 30, Gary Yim 14.

Every attempt has been made to clear copyright. Should there be any
inadvertent omission please apply to the publisher for rectification.

Contents

Right now, there are around 7 billion people living on Earth. Sixty years ago, there were just 2.5 billion. In less than the lifespan of the average human, the world's population – the number of people living on the planet – has gone up by an amazing 4.5 billion.

A ticking time bomb?

According to the United Nations, around 134 million babies are born each year. If this continues, in 100 years from now there could be twice the number of people in the world as there are today.

FACE FACTS

'Humans everywhere must understand that rapid population growth damages the Earth and diminishes human well-being.'
David Pimentel, Professor Emeritus at Cornell University

Africa is one of the areas in which the population is rising at incredible rates.

Of the world's 7 billion people, 4.5 billion (60 per cent) live in Asia.

DIFFERENT VIEWPOINTS

Some experts think that there are far too many people on the planet. They say that if the population keeps rising at current rates, we will one day run out of food, clean water and other resources, such as oil, coal and gas. Other experts disagree. They believe that instead of increasing, in the future the world's population will decrease.

BIG QUESTIONS

So, should we be worried? Are there too many people living on Earth? If there are, what can we do to change the situation? In this book, we ask the experts for answers to these questions. We'll then ask you to become the expert and make up your own mind about our growing population crisis.

ask the experts

MANY EXPERTS SAY THAT IT IS NOT JUST THE WORLD POPULATION WE NEED TO BE CONCERNED ABOUT, BUT THE GROWING POPULATIONS IN OUR CITIES. MORE AND MORE PEOPLE ARE MOVING TO CITIES. WE URGENTLY NEED TO BUILD MORE CITY HOUSING TO COPE WITH THE DEMAND OF AN EVER-GROWING POPULATION.

Every year, more and more people are being born around the world. Added to this, in the West most people are now living for longer than ever before. Our longer lifespans are putting further pressure on resources, such as food, oil and gas. The question is, will Earth be able to provide enough resources for a potentially huge future population?

A global crisis

Parents in the West can expect their children to live longer than them, thanks to advances in healthcare.

Better health

So why are we living longer? There are two main reasons. The first is the increase in the quality of healthcare. Over the last 100 years, doctors and scientists have found ways to cure many diseases. The invention of vaccines to protect us against disease, and of new methods to treat other illnesses, has cut death rates dramatically.

As more people live long, healthy lives, the number of people on Earth will continue to rise.

More food

Most people around the world are also healthier because the quality of their diets has improved and they also consume more food. This is because of changes in the way we grow and harvest food crops. The 'Green Revolution' of the 1960s and 1970s made food cheaper to produce and buy than ever before for people in the developed world. Because of this, fewer people go hungry and die of starvation than in the past.

" THE DEBATE

Experts are divided on the impact of the 'Green Revolution' in farming. Some think that in the future it will become too expensive to produce as much food as we do now, and people will starve. Norman Barlaug, the man credited with driving the 'Green Revolution', disagrees. He says it has been 'a change in the right direction' and 'transformed the world'. "

A FARMING CRISIS?

As the world's population increases, it puts greater pressure on Earth's natural resources. At present, fewer people than ever before in Earth's history go hungry. However, the food we produce is not evenly distributed and in some parts of the world people still starve. Some experts think that if the population keeps increasing, by 2030 there might not be enough food to feed everyone.

FACE FACTS

'Our food reserves are at a 50-year low, and by 2030 we need to be producing 50 per cent more food. If not, many people will starve.' Professor John Beddington, Government Chief Scientist for the United Kingdom

Asian farmers currently produce around 454 tonnes of rice every year, but will they be able to produce more in the future?

These people are begging for food at a refugee camp in Africa. More people in Africa and Asia may starve if we do not find ways to grow more food.

RUNNING OUT OF LAND

Today, around 12 per cent of the land available on Earth is used for growing food. However, experts say there is only an additional 13 per cent of land available to grow more food in the future. If we do not find ways to increase production within the land we already farm, people may starve.

POSSIBLE SOLUTIONS

Some experts have suggested that the way forward is to build skyscrapers in which food is grown. Others say that people in rich countries should eat and waste less food. At present, people in the United Kingdom throw away 15 million tonnes of edible food each year. Many say that we should distribute the food more fairly around the world.

" THE DEBATE

Some experts deny that there is a growing food crisis. In 2000, population experts Michael Haynes and Rumy Hussan wrote: 'In a world that now produces more food than is necessary to feed all its population, there is no excuse for hunger.' However, many others disagree. They point out that we already use 90 per cent of the land that can be farmed, and demand for food will soon be too great for many farmers to cope. "

Demand for oil is growing in countries such as India, where the population is rising.

A FUEL CRISIS

Demand for natural fuels, such as oil, gas and coal, has risen sharply in recent years. This is because of the increasing numbers of people on Earth. Fuel is needed to power the farming equipment and factories that produce our food. It is also needed to provide power for aeroplanes and cars, generate electricity and heat homes. As the world's population increases, people are using up Earth's natural fuels more quickly than ever before. We are simply using too much, too quickly for Earth to cope.

ask the experts

MOST EXPERTS AGREE THAT OIL WILL RUN OUT AT SOME POINT. THEY ARE ALSO CONCERNED THAT, AS OIL RUNS OUT, PRICES WILL SOAR. WHEN THAT HAPPENS, IT WILL BECOME MUCH MORE EXPENSIVE TO PRODUCE AND TRANSPORT FOOD. AS A RESULT, FOOD WILL BECOME MORE EXPENSIVE TO BUY. THIS WILL PUT FURTHER STRAIN ON THE WORLD'S GROWING POPULATION, AND COULD EVEN LEAD TO RIOTS OR WARS.

OIL ISSUES

Gas, coal and oil cannot be made by people. They come from 'reserves' deep underground. We already use many of these reserves, and one day, they will run out. Unless we work out other ways to farm food, generate electricity and power transport, we will face an enormous future energy crisis.

FACE FACTS

'We have enough oil for the next few years. After that, the situation deteriorates.'
Chris Skrebowski, Editor, *Petroleum Review*

IS TIME RUNNING OUT?

Exactly how much oil is left in the ground is a matter of great debate. A report by the oil industry in 2007 predicted that there is enough to last another 40 years, but only if the amount we use each year does not increase. As the world's population grows, it is likely we will use more and Earth's oil wells will have run dry before 2050.

Experts are all agreed that we must find alternatives to our current energy supplies, such as oil from offshore oil rigs.

A PLANET IN CRISIS

Experts claim that we are damaging Earth almost beyond repair. To house and feed everyone, we have cut down forests to build more cities, plundered the planet's natural resources and built factories that spew toxic gases into the air. As a result, we are running out of usable land, many species of animals and plants have died out and stocks of natural materials that are needed for building are dwindling very quickly.

GLOBAL WARMING

Some scientists also believe that the huge number of people now using oil as a fuel is contributing to 'global warming', which is making the world's weather more extreme. As a result of global warming, experts say that parts of the world are drying out, making it difficult for crops to grow, while storms and floods are drenching other areas.

Experts fear that our effect on the planet is now causing natural disasters such as hurricanes.

FACE FACTS

'The human impact on the planet could be the loss of all species by the end of the twenty-first century.' Peter Raven, former President of the American Association for the Advancement of Science

Experts say that global warming caused by our reliance on oil is melting the ice at the top and bottom of the planet.

FRAGILE WORLD

Scientists point out that for the planet to remain a healthy place for humans to live, we need to protect wildlife. We need plants and trees to supply us with oxygen to breathe. By forcing species into extinction we will disrupt the natural balance of life on our planet. Some scientists believe we have already exceeded the 'carrying capacity' of Earth – the number of people the planet can sustain without being damaged beyond repair forever.

" THE DEBATE

Not all scientists agree that humans are to blame for global warming. Some say it is part of a natural increase in the planet's temperature over many millions of years. "

In Brazil, many people live together in poorly-built shacks in areas called 'favelas'.

askthe experts

A HOUSING CRISIS

Two of the most pressing problems linked to overpopulation are poverty and overcrowding. If someone is living in poverty, it means they are so poor they do not have enough money to buy food or proper shelter. In many places around the world, a large part of the population lives in poverty. They are forced to live on the streets, or crowd into tiny, run-down homes. These homes are often made of whatever can be found, from pieces of concrete and wood to sections of plastic and sheets of corrugated iron.

SHANTYTOWNS

Overcrowding is a problem in many cities around the world. In certain parts of Asia, Africa and South America, poor people are forced to live in 'shantytowns'. These are large areas full of poorly constructed and crowded housing, barely fit for people to live in. Disease is widespread. According to recent figures, more than 1 billion people worldwide live in shantytowns.

SHIFTING THE PROBLEM

Some people in developing countries are prepared to move to richer countries in the hope of finding a better life. This in turn leads to more overcrowded cities, more disease and more problems. These problems will just get worse as the world's population increases in size over the years.

ONE PROBLEM REPLACES ANOTHER

The dream of a better life in a new country is not always fulfilled. Many of the people who have travelled from developing countries to developed countries have found themselves living in poor conditions. Sometimes, their new lives are hardly better than those they left behind.

Many people move to the United Kingdom each year in search of work and a better life.

FACE FACTS

'An ever-growing demand for resources by a growing population is threatening our future security, health and well-being.'
Jim Leape,
International Director,
World Wildlife Fund

While population numbers have been increasing all over the world, the most dramatic rises have been seen in what we call the 'developing world', traditionally poor countries in places such as Africa, Asia and some parts of South America.

A developing crisis

In some African countries, the population has increased by 40 or 50 per cent in less than 10 years. The African state of Chad had a population of just over 6 million in 1993. In 2009, it topped 10 million for the first time.

In poor African countries, the lack of food sometimes results in famine and people are forced to rely on refugee camps, such as this one.

FACE FACTS

'It remains a brutal fact that human population growth will stop at some point. That can happen by fewer births, or by an increased death rate. There is, alas, no third alternative of indefinite growth.'
Sir David Attenborough, journalist and wildlife expert

Africa's rapid population growth has led to an increased number of people living in makeshift shelters, such as these.

HEALTHCARE MIRACLE

So why has the population rise been greatest in the developing world? As in other parts of the world, greater access to healthcare there has meant that many people are living longer. This, coupled with a massive increase in the number of children being born, has led to the population of some countries spiralling out of control.

Children in Africa face severe health and social problems as a result of overcrowding.

MASS POVERTY

Many developing world countries do not have the money or facilities to cope with rapid population growth. Most people are poor, and there is often not enough housing, food and clean water for everyone. Because of this, disease and death are rife. Yet, even when large numbers of people die, the population keeps on growing unchecked.

ask the experts

EXPERTS SAY THAT ONE OF THE MAIN REASONS SO MANY CHILDREN ARE BEING BORN IN DEVELOPING WORLD COUNTRIES IS A LACK OF KNOWLEDGE ABOUT WHAT WE CALL 'BIRTH CONTROL'. OPPOSITION TO BIRTH CONTROL FROM SOME RELIGIOUS LEADERS ALSO PLAYS A BIG PART.

17

India in crisis

Nowhere in the world is population growth more out of control than in India. In 1951, the population stood at a sizeable 361.7 million. Sixty years later, in 2011, that had grown to 1.2 billion, an increase of 245 per cent.

There are now simply too many people in the country to feed, water, clothe and shelter. If India's population keeps growing at its current rate, 1.7 billion people will live there by 2030. This will be the largest population of any country on Earth. Will the country be able to cope with this enormous population?

FACE FACTS

'Humans are 10,000 times more common than we should be.' Steve Jones, Head of the Department of Biology at University College, London

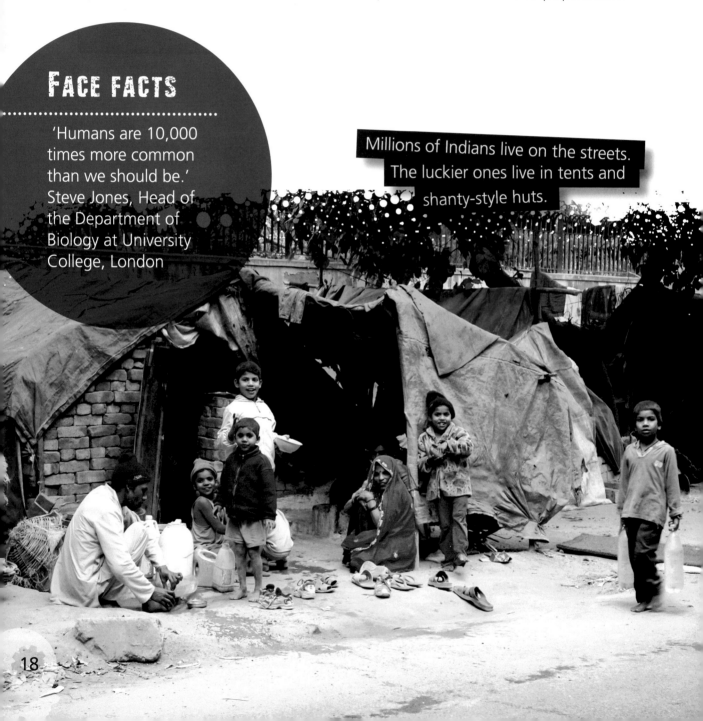

Millions of Indians live on the streets. The luckier ones live in tents and shanty-style huts.

Mass population, mass misery

Overcrowding in India has already resulted in huge areas of slum housing in its cities, mass starvation and a high rate of death in babies and children. There is also mass unemployment, no education for millions of children and no healthcare for the majority of people who live in the country. Although there are wealthy sections in India's population, overpopulation and poverty mean misery for many millions of Indians.

The future for India

Unless population growth is controlled in India, the outlook is bleak. Some other countries have started taking steps to cut birth rates. Will India now have to follow suit, too?

Around 70,000 babies are born In India each day.

ask the experts

POPULATION EXPERTS AGREE THAT THE ONLY WAY TO CONTROL THE POPULATION GROWTH IS TO LIMIT BIRTH RATES IN AREAS SUCH AS INDIA, WHERE IT IS OUT OF CONTROL. WE WILL LOOK AT HOW THIS MAY BE DONE, AND WHAT HAPPENED WHEN CHINA TRIED THIS METHOD OF POPULATION CONTROL, LATER IN THIS BOOK.

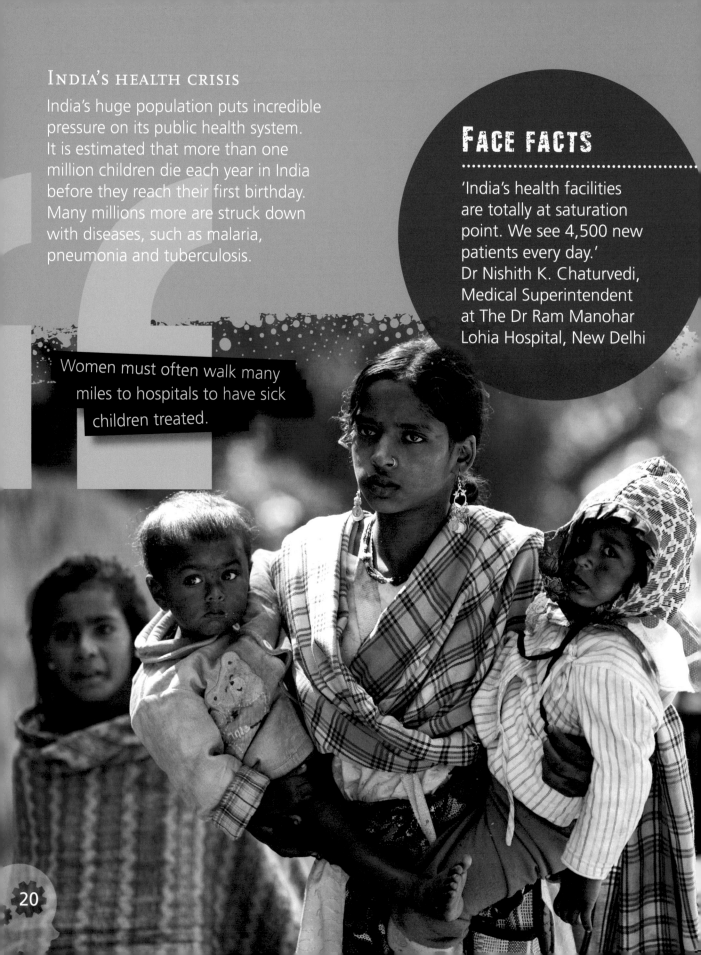

INDIA'S HEALTH CRISIS

India's huge population puts incredible pressure on its public health system. It is estimated that more than one million children die each year in India before they reach their first birthday. Many millions more are struck down with diseases, such as malaria, pneumonia and tuberculosis.

FACE FACTS

'India's health facilities are totally at saturation point. We see 4,500 new patients every day.' Dr Nishith K. Chaturvedi, Medical Superintendent at The Dr Ram Manohar Lohia Hospital, New Delhi

Women must often walk many miles to hospitals to have sick children treated.

The poor on the streets of India have no access to doctors.

Far too little, too late

Sickness and disease are major problems in India, because so many people live in poverty and have little access to medical treatment. Death rates from curable diseases are worst in remote, rural areas. To get treatment, people are often forced to travel for many miles to find a hospital. India's health system is stretched to the breaking point.

Fighting back

India has shown that it is capable of fighting back against disease and poverty. In 2012, India's prime minister announced that in the past year not a single new case of polio had been recorded. Polio is a deadly disease that had already been wiped out in most of the world. India is now polio-free for the first time in history.

ask the experts

HEALTH EXPERTS AGREE THAT MILLIONS OF CHILDREN WILL KEEP DYING IN INDIA EVERY YEAR UNLESS THE GOVERNMENT COMMITS BILLIONS MORE POUNDS TO FIGHTING CONDITIONS SUCH AS MALNUTRITION, TUBERCULOSIS AND MALARIA. AS MANY OF THESE DISEASES HAVE SIMPLY BUILT UP A RESISTANCE TO THE DRUGS CURRENTLY USED TO FIGHT THEM, IT WILL MEAN DEVELOPING NEW VACCINES, FAST.

Giant effort

India's success in eradicating polio is due to a huge effort from the government, medical services and global charities. More than £600 million has been spent on making and delivering polio vaccines. Doctors and charity workers were sent to the most remote parts of the country to give vaccine injections to children. The process took a huge amount of time and effort, but it has been a great success.

Millions of Africans suffer from HIV/AIDS, yet have very little healthcare to support them.

AFRICA IN CRISIS

Despite all of India's problems, its economy is developing rapidly and the government has money to spend on healthcare programs. The same cannot be said for many countries in Africa, where population growth, overcrowding and poverty are almost as bad. There, many Africans face a daily struggle for survival. Many women give birth to a high number of children during their lives, but living conditions are so bad in some places that several of these children may die before they even reach just five years of age.

RISING BIRTH RATES

Although more people are born in India and China every year than anywhere else on Earth, birth rates are actually far higher in central, western and northern African countries. This is because birth rate figures are calculated on the number of births per 1,000 people, rather than just the number of people born. This means that, in Africa, more babies are being born to fewer women.

Out of control

The population growth in Africa over the last 60 years has been simply staggering. In 1950, the continent was home to around 230 million people. In 2010, that number stood at more than 1 billion. The rate shows no signs of slowing, either. In the 10 years between 2000 and 2010, the continent's population grew by more than 25 per cent.

Birth rates in many African countries are much higher than in India or China.

ask the experts

MOST EXPERTS AGREE THAT THE ROOT OF AFRICA'S POPULATION PROBLEMS IS POVERTY. UNLESS THE STANDARD OF LIVING OF POOR AFRICANS IS INCREASED, AND MORE PEOPLE ARE EDUCATED, BIRTH RATES WILL CONTINUE TO RISE AND AFRICA WILL FACE AN ENORMOUS FUTURE CRISIS.

FAMINE IN AFRICA

Many experts worry about the problems of overpopulation in Africa, because of the continent's unique natural difficulties. The continent is one of the hottest places on Earth. This means that much of the soil is dry, full of rocks and hard to grow crops in. Clean, fresh water is also scarce. Droughts cause local rivers, water holes and lakes to dry up.

These harsh conditions mean that famines, where hundreds of thousands of people go hungry, are common.

FACE FACTS

'The economic situation has brought it home to our people that if they want their children to be educated and well fed, then they have to begin to do something about the amount of children they have.'
Olikoye Ransome-Kuti, former Minister of Health, Nigeria

When famine strikes Africa, many children go hungry unless their families reach refugee camps at which food and help can be found.

In refugee relief camps, children are at risk of catching deadly diseases, such as malaria and cholera.

MAJOR CRISIS

When famine or drought hits an African country, the results can be devastating. The international community does what it can to help, offering money, food and water. But the stark truth is that there are far too many people starving, or dying of dehydration, for charities and aid agencies to help. The reality is that little can be done to avoid the deaths of thousands.

DEATH AND DISEASE

When famine strikes an African country, many people travel for hundreds of miles to find relief. When they reach their destination, there is usually nowhere for them to sleep. Charities try to help by setting up huge refugee relief camps. However, the conditions in these camps are often terrible. It is not uncommon for people to die in the camps from diseases picked up by living in dirty conditions, close to sick people.

ask the experts

EXPERTS SAY THAT ONE OF THE BEST WAYS TO COMBAT POVERTY AND OVERPOPULATION IN AFRICA IS TO EDUCATE MORE CHILDREN. AT PRESENT, MILLIONS OF AFRICAN CHILDREN HAVE NO ACCESS TO SCHOOLING. IF THEY WERE EDUCATED, THEY WOULD HAVE GREATER PROSPECTS AND BE ABLE TO MAKE BETTER CHOICES.

It is easy to look at the problems population growth causes in the developing world and think it is not our problem. Yet experts say overpopulation is a very real issue for almost every country on Earth, even in developed nations, such as the United Kingdom, United States and Australia.

A developed world problem

In the West, immigration, a growing population and a shrinking job market mean that even low-skill jobs are now in demand.

FACE FACTS

'A doubling in population will plunge us into an age of extinction and desolation unseen since the dinosaurs disappeared 65 million years ago.'
Chris Hedges, journalist and author

The West is now feeling the impact of a growing population, with fewer jobs and greater poverty.

"THE DEBATE

Some experts believe that population growth is linked to the easy availability of food. They say that when food is cheap and plentiful, the population rises. Other experts do not agree. They point out that the population is growing fastest in poorer countries, where there is less food. Also, the population of rich European countries such as Germany is expected to fall in the next 30 years. "

BLAME GAME

Some experts argue that the world's population crisis is not the fault of people in Africa or Asia, but of the developed world. Some scientists in these richer nations have driven advances in healthcare and the mass production of food. It is the people in these wealthier nations, too, who consume most of the world's precious natural resources.

CRITICAL MASS

Birth rates are actually falling in the developed world, but that has not stopped population growth because we live longer. For example, the population of North America (the United States and Canada combined) has increased by 25 per cent since 1950. In Europe, it has increased by 10 per cent. In the West, we are as much to blame for the world's rapidly growing population as developing countries.

Could our population growth mean that jobs, food and money in the United Kingdom could be in short supply?

FACE FACTS

'If there ever is a time of plenty, this will automatically lead to an increase in the population until the natural state of starvation and misery is restored.'
Professor Richard Dawkins, University of Oxford
.

UNITED KINGDOM IN CRISIS?

The population of the United Kingdom is on the rise, with a population that is growing three times faster than any other country within Europe. The United Kingdom now has a population of around 63 million people and the population has grown by 3.1 million since 2001. Some experts say that the country is becoming dangerously overcrowded, with cities practically bursting at the seams. They are very concerned that in the future there will not be enough food, jobs or money for every citizen within the country.

RISING AND RISING

Current figures, published by the Office for National Statistics, show that the UK population will grow to 65.6 million by 2018 and will reach 70 million by 2029. By 2083, the figure will rise to almost 86 million – and is then projected to continue to grow by more than one-quarter of a million people each year.

Immigration and old age

One of the reasons for the projected increase in the number of people living in the United Kingdom is simple – immigration. More than half (54 per cent) of the increase in the UK population between 1991 and 2012 was due to immigration. People are also living longer, which is adding to population growth in the country.

As the UK population continues to grow, will more people be forced to live on the streets?

ask the experts

Experts agree that if the United Kingdom does not control its population growth, the country could struggle to support all of its people in the future. Even basic needs, such as supplying people with enough food and water, could be impossible to fulfil. The gap between the richest and poorest people will increase, and social unrest is likely to follow.

More than our fair share

The overuse of resources in many Western countries is also putting our planet under pressure. As the largest Western country, the United States in particular uses enormous quantities of natural resources – almost twice as many as it produces. Americans own 30 per cent of all the cars in the world, pump more toxic gases into Earth's atmosphere and use up more than 20 per cent of the oil produced in the world each year. What's more, the average American uses 400 litres of water every day, compared to the 10 litres used by people in the world's developing countries.

No way back

Population experts say these statistics are unsustainable. This means that people in developed countries such as the United States cannot continue to use up the world's resources so quickly. We are taking more than our fair share, and it is time to reconsider.

Due to excessive consumption, the average American produces 68 tonnes of rubbish by the time they are 75 years old.

Face Facts

'Infinite growth of consumption in a finite world is an impossibility.'
E. F. Schumacher, economist and writer

Our Western obsession with the latest goods is driving us to overconsumption and eventual self-destruction.

OVERCONSUMPTION

Excessive consumption of natural resources is called overconsumption. Experts believe that as the world's population continues to grow, the problem of overconsumption in rich nations will reach crisis levels. More people on Earth means more demand for food, fuel and water. Unless the West can cut down its consumption of resources, more people will die in Africa, Asia and poor parts of South America. Eventually, the West will starve, too.

ask the experts

MOST EXPERTS AGREE THAT THE ONLY SOLUTION TO OVERCONSUMPTION IN DEVELOPED COUNTRIES IS TO SLOW THE RATE AT WHICH WE ARE USING UP RESOURCES, SUCH AS OIL AND NATURAL GAS. HOWEVER, THIS WOULD REQUIRE NEW LAWS FROM GOVERNMENTS. THESE WOULD BE VERY UNPOPULAR WITH MOST PEOPLE, AND IT IS VERY UNLIKELY WE WILL SEE THEM IN THE NEAR FUTURE.

Grain mountains (huge stores of grain) in the West and no food for people in developing countries – is this fair?

UNPOPULAR SOLUTIONS

Governments around the world realise that rich countries must reduce their consumption of natural resources, in response to the growing population crisis. Some experts think that the only way to slow down population growth is to lift poor countries out of poverty. That means allowing them to use more resources, while richer countries in the West must use fewer.

IMPORTANT AGREEMENT

Since the late 1990s, many governments around the world have been trying to reach an agreement to reduce the amount of energy they use. In 2005, an agreement was reached in Japan in which most of the world's governments agreed to cut down their energy use. Only one major nation would not sign the Kyoto Protocol – the United States.

FACE FACTS

'Each American puts out about 18 tonnes of carbon dioxide gases every year. Somehow, we have to make changes that will bring that down to zero.' Bill Gates, founder, Microsoft

Big failure

The idea behind the Kyoto Protocol was that developed countries would limit the amount of harmful gases they released into the air through their oil refineries and other factories. To do so, developed countries would use less oil and save precious oil resources for future use. It would also mean that fewer harmful gases would be released into the atmosphere, to counter those released by developing countries as their industries increase.

ask the experts

MANY EXPERTS HAVE QUESTIONED THE SUCCESS OF THE KYOTO PROTOCOL. THEY SAY THAT BECAUSE THE US GOVERNMENT DID NOT SIGN UP, IT WILL BE DOOMED TO FAILURE. UNLESS THE UNITED STATES RADICALLY REDUCES ITS CONSUMPTION OF ENERGY, OTHER COUNTRIES MAY BACK OUT OF THE AGREEMENT, AND WE WILL BE NO FURTHER FORWARD.

Using wind to generate electricity rather than oil, gas or coal could be one answer to our energy problems.

The world's growing population is like a ticking bomb. For every year that we continue to do nothing to stop it, we get nearer to catastrophe.

Radical solutions

Population experts say that the time for simple action has passed. We need to think about more radical solutions to solve Earth's population crisis.

FACE FACTS

'Those who oppose birth control are either incapable of arithmetic or in favour of war and famine as permanent features of human life.' Bertrand Russell, philosopher

Experts say that reducing the number of babies people have is the key to tackling population growth.

TWO KEY AIMS

Experts agree that there are two things that need to be done to avert disaster and slow down the population explosion. The first, as we have seen, is to share the world's resources more fairly. That means persuading people in wealthy nations to reduce the resources that they use. The second is somehow to control the growing number of people who are being born around the world.

A DIFFICULT PROBLEM

Slowing the birth rate is not easy. One way to do it is to make everyone richer, as statistics show that birth rates are falling rapidly in the world's wealthiest countries. However, this method would take many, many years, possibly even a century. Other methods that would get quicker results include better education about family planning, and laws to limit the number of children people can have.

Governments may have to take drastic action to stop people from having a lot of children.

ask the experts

POPULATION EXPERTS HAVE BEEN ADVISING FOR YEARS THAT WE MUST SLOW DOWN BIRTH RATES AROUND THE WORLD. THE QUESTION IS, ARE OUR GOVERNMENTS LISTENING? MOST GOVERNMENTS ARE UNCOMFORTABLE WITH SPENDING MORE MONEY ON BIRTH CONTROL, OR INTRODUCING LAWS THAT PREVENT PEOPLE FROM MAKING A CHOICE ABOUT THE NUMBER OF CHILDREN THAT THEY HAVE.

CHINA'S SOLUTION

China is the most highly populated country on the planet, with well over 1.3 billion people. That figure would be even higher if the country's communist government had not introduced its highly controversial population control policies in 1979. Between then and 2013, Chinese couples living in towns and cities were banned from having more than just one child.

DRASTIC MEASURES

China's 'one child policy' was introduced after the country's population almost doubled in the 30 years between 1949 and 1979. The government was worried about the effects of overpopulation in cities, so decided to allow married couples to have only one child. Today, the policy remains in place, but has been relaxed slightly so that families in which one parent is a single child may now have two children. The government says its policy has prevented 200–300 million births, but many doubt that this is true.

"THE DEBATE

So has the one child policy been a success? The Chinese government claims that it has reduced problems associated with overpopulation. However, critics say that the policy will have created a new problem in the future – once the parents of one child families grow old, there will simply not be enough children to care for them. "

China decided to introduce population control measures to combat its overpopulation problems.

Is China's one child policy a solution to overpopulation, or is it a problem instead?

SUCCESS OR FAILURE?

Since China's one child policy was introduced, birth rates have fallen significantly. However, critics point out that as China's population is still growing fast, the policy has not been a success. They say it has also led to more secret births, and the brutal treatment of couples that break the ban.

FACE FACTS

'China's population is ageing fast. The first children born under the one child policy face the prospect of caring for an ever-increasing number of old people. The clock is ticking.'
Weiliang Nie,
BBC China Service

The birth control issue

Few countries are willing to follow China's example by forcibly limiting the number of children people have. Many, however, are looking more closely at the issues of birth control and family planning. Many Western couples think carefully about how many children to have, and when. Now countries such as India are encouraging their citizens to do the same.

Face facts

'We are given two choices to deal with overpopulation – famine, pestilence and war on one hand, birth control on the other. Most of us choose birth control.'
Aldous Huxley, writer

The use of contraceptives could be a solution to India's growing population crisis.

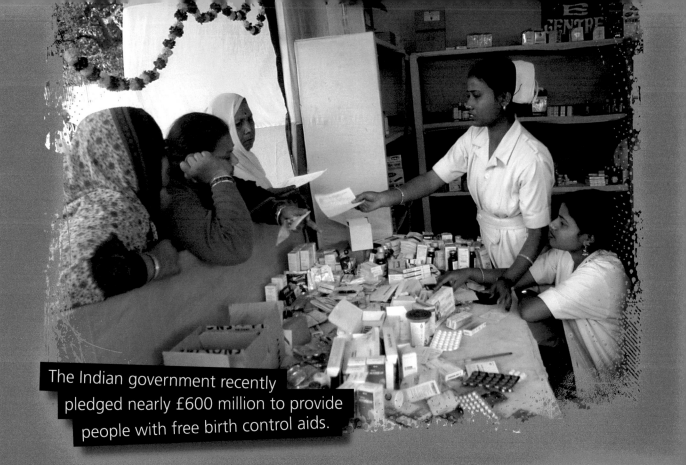

The Indian government recently pledged nearly £600 million to provide people with free birth control aids.

FAMILY PLANNING

Birth control is the process of reducing the number of births by encouraging people to use contraception. Using contraception stops a woman from becoming pregnant. In some countries, contraceptives are given out free of charge, to reduce the number of unwanted pregnancies.

CHURCH OBJECTIONS

Although contraceptives are widely used worldwide, they are frowned upon by some religions. United Nations officers report hearing Muslim leaders in Africa telling people not to use contraceptives, while the Catholic Church is also strongly opposed to contraception.

ask the experts

POPULATION EXPERTS AGREE THAT BIRTH CONTROL IS THE QUICKEST WAY TO SLOW DOWN POPULATION GROWTH AROUND THE WORLD. THEY SAY THAT IT IS VITAL TO EDUCATE PEOPLE IN DEVELOPING NATIONS ABOUT FAMILY PLANNING AND CONTRACEPTIVES. THIS WAY, THEY MIGHT CHOOSE TO HAVE FEWER CHILDREN. THIS IS SOMETHING THAT MANY PEOPLE IN DEVELOPED COUNTRIES IN THE WEST ARE ALREADY DOING.

The politics of population

Over recent years, many population experts, scientists and writers have called on governments worldwide to act now to stop Earth's population from spiralling out of control. Yet governments have mostly done very little. So why are they not listening to expert warnings?

Immigration is becoming a subject much debated by politicians such as Nigel Farage as jobs and resources are put under increasing pressure.

Controversial ideas

Many of the solutions proposed to slow down population growth are controversial. They mostly require people to limit their use of natural resources or the number of children they have. While these types of laws may be needed to avert a crisis in 50 or 100 years' time, most politicians only think in the short term. They are concerned about getting re-elected at the next election. Introducing these measures would be unpopular, and no politician will risk policies that could lose votes.

Face facts

'The chief cause for the impending collapse of the world is the enormous growth of the human population. The worst enemy of life is too much life.' Pentti Linkola, ecologist and writer

No action in the West

In Western countries, there is little likelihood of politicians passing new birth control, immigration or energy-saving laws in the near future. Most people in Western countries would be opposed to such laws and any politician who introduced them would be unlikely to be re-elected. It is also likely that any proposed laws would face opposition from many religious groups.

ask the experts

MOST POPULATION EXPERTS BELIEVE THAT THE TIME FOR GOVERNMENT ACTION ON POPULATION IS NOW. THEY SAY THAT A FAILURE TO INTRODUCE LAWS AND POLICIES TO SLOW POPULATION GROWTH WOULD DOOM HUMAN LIFE TO ALMOST CERTAIN EXTINCTION. HOWEVER, FEW BELIEVE GOVERNMENTS WILL ACTUALLY TAKE ANY ACTION, DESPITE THE EXPERT EVIDENCE THAT BACKS UP THEIR CLAIMS.

Will Western governments ever limit the number of children that people have?

ROOM FOR MORE?

For all the doom, gloom and warnings of harsh times ahead, not all experts agree that overpopulation is a problem. Some even argue that Earth can cope with far more people without being damaged beyond repair. Is this really the case? According to a United Nations report in 2003, the world population will peak in 2050. After that, it will stay at the same level until 2300. Other experts predict that after 2050, the world's population will start falling as a natural response to overpopulation.

A few experts say there is no problem with overpopulation, in Africa or elsewhere.

Some scientists have proposed leaving Earth altogether, to set up homes elsewhere on other planets.

CONTROVERSIAL IDEAS

Other experts disagree strongly with this opinion. They have urged the world to look for more radical solutions. One such solution is sterilisation – the process of making people infertile, so they are incapable of producing offspring. Some highly controversial scientists have suggested a system of sterilisation in which people have just one or two children. It is a radical proposal and has little support.

SPACE SOLUTION

In the 1970s, a small group of scientists in the United States came up with another extreme solution to the problem – setting up new homes on other planets. In 1999, a scientist called Gerard Freeman proposed setting up 'human colonies' in space. He believes this could happen within centuries, although very few other scientists currently agree with him.

ask the experts

POPULATION EXPERT DR ALEX BERZOW DOES NOT BELIEVE THAT OVERPOPULATION IS A MAJOR ISSUE. HE SAYS THAT AS COUNTRIES SUCH AS INDIA AND CHINA DEVELOP AND BEGIN TO GET RICHER, THEIR PEOPLE WILL ENJOY THE BENEFITS OF THIS NEW WEALTH, AND POPULATION RISES WILL NATURALLY BEGIN TO SLOW.

So, which side are you on? Is the rapid growth of the human population putting the very survival of Earth at risk, or are scientists worrying about nothing? Do we need to think of radical solutions to a growing crisis, or can we just let nature take its course?

You're the expert

Do you think it is right to control immigration for the sake of population control in the United States?

FACE FACTS

'The truth is that the population bomb is being defused around the world. But the consumption bomb is still primed and ever more dangerous.' Fred Pearce, author, *Peoplequake*

Running out of time?

The arguments for action on population growth are very strong. For thousands of years, the human population of Earth could be counted in millions, rather than billions. There are now 6 billion more humans on Earth than there were 100 years ago. The planet has only a limited amount of natural resources. Do you think the human race can continue to use up Earth's resources and still be around in a few thousand years' time?

Can we solve mass poverty in developing countries by reducing consumption in the West?

"THE DEBATE

One of the most vocal opponents of the idea of overpopulation is a group called the Population Research Institute (PRI). They say that overpopulation is a myth, created by some scientists to push through their personal beliefs. Scientists have hit back, pointing out that the PRI is funded not by scientific institutions, but by religious organisations that are against birth control. "

Nothing to worry about?

On the other side of the debate, scientists point out that the human race has overcome a lot of obstacles in the last 2,000 years. We are inventive and adaptable, and will find new ways to grow food and produce more energy, such as harnessing the power of the sun, water or wind. Do you think we will find answers to our population growth and find ways to live sustainably? If you were the expert, what would you decide?

Glossary

birth control measures used to limit the number of children people have

brutal severe

calculated worked out

charities organisations set up to raise money in order to help people who are poor or sick

consumption using goods or services, for example food, fuel or water

contraception the process of stopping women from having children by use of contraceptives (see below)

contraceptives medicines or other methods used to prevent women getting pregnant

developing world a term used to describe poorer, less developed countries, usually in places such as Africa and Asia

drought a long period of low rainfall that results in the drying up of natural water resources such as rivers and lakes

edible safe to eat

educated sent to school to learn to read and write

election the process of selecting a government, where people vote for their preferred politicians

eradicating destroying or getting rid of something, for example a deadly disease

exceeded gone past an agreed limit

extinction when the last of a species of animal or plant dies out

family planning the process of deciding when to have children, and how many

famine what happens when a country cannot produce enough food to feed its population, usually because of severe heat or other extreme weather conditions

finite limited

global warming rising world temperatures, contributed to by the burning of fossil fuels, which may be causing extreme weather

Green Revolution the development in agricultural technology between the 1940s and 1960s that helped farmers produce more food

life expectancy how long someone is expected to live

overpopulation when there are too many people in a certain place and not enough money, food, water or homes for everyone

plundered taken a lot of something

politician a person who is chosen by the people of a country to make decisions and to represent them in government

population the number of people living in a certain place

population control measures taken to limit the number of people in a certain country or region, for example limiting the number of children that people can have

poverty not having enough money to live to an acceptable standard

projections forecasts or predictions of what may happen in the future, based on known facts

radical extreme

refugee relief camps temporary camps set up to provide food, water and shelter for people who have lost their homes because of war, famine or drought

United Nations a worldwide organisation with representatives from all countries

vaccines medicines given to people to stop them from catching certain diseases

Books

Coping with Population Growth (The Environment Challenge), Nicola Barber, Raintree

Material World: A Global Family Portrait, Peter Menzel and Charles C. Mann, Sierra Club Books

The World in One Day (Incredible Comparisons), Russell Ash, Dorling Kindersley

For more information

Websites

How many people are there currently on Earth? Find out at:
www.census.gov/popclock

National Geographic has a special website looking at the issue of population. Are there too many people on Earth? Find out at:
http://ngm.nationalgeographic.com/7-billion

Find out more about overpopulation at:
http://encyclopedia.kids.net.au/page/ov/Overpopulation

Note to parents and teachers
Every effort has been made by the Publisher to ensure that these websites contain no inappropriate or offensive material. However, because of the nature of the Internet, it is impossible to guarantee that the contents of these sites will not be altered. We strongly advise that Internet access is supervised by a responsible adult.

Index